TEENS SPEAK
BOYS AGES 16 to 18

Sixty Original Character Monologues

by Kristen Dabrowski

KIDS SPEAK SERIES

A Smith and Kraus Book

A Smith and Kraus Book
Published by Smith and Kraus, Inc.
177 Lyme Road, Hanover, NH 03755
www.smithkraus.com

LIMITED REPRODUCTION PERMISSION
The publisher grants permission to individual teachers
to reproduce the scripts as needed for use with their own students.
Permission for reproduction for an entire school district
or for commercial use is required. Please call Smith and Kraus
at (603) 643-6431.

First Edition: March 2005
Manufactured in the United States of America
10 9 8 7 6 5 4 3 2 1

Cover and text design by Julia Gignoux, Freedom Hill Design
Library of Congress Cataloging-in-Publication
Dabrowski, Kristen.
Boys speak, ages 16–18 ; sixty character monologues / by Kristen Dabrowski.
—1st ed.
p. cm. — (Kids speak series)
ISBN 1-57525-415-8
1. Monologues. 2. Acting. I. Title: Boys speak, ages sixteen to eighteen. II. Title:
Boys speak, ages sixteen through eighteen. III. Title. IV. Series.

PN2080.D334 2005
812'.6—dc22
200405045

CONTENTS

To my favorite teachers,
who allowed me to speak my mind

Foreword

Hello, actors! Inside this book, you'll find sixty monologues for boys aged 16 to 18.

Here's how they are organized:

- There are six sections in the book. Each section includes ten monologues from the point of view of one character. Each character is described on his own introduction page.

- Each character was designed to have different experiences and views on the world. You'll see him in school, at home, with strangers, etc.

How to choose a monologue:

- You may want to begin by looking at the character descriptions. Choose a character most like you or, for a challenge, choose one that is quite different from yourself.

- Page through the monologues. There are dramatic, comic, and semicomic monologues in each section. Some characters are more comic or dramatic than others.

- Trust your instincts!

How to perform the monologues:

- Tell your story clearly.

- Know to whom you're speaking and imagine you are talking to just that one person. (Of course, if you're talking to more people, keep that in mind as well!)

- A new paragraph or *(Beat.)* means that there is a pause due to a subject change or another (imaginary) person speaking. Be sure that you know what the unseen person is saying.

- Play around with the monologue and try doing it a lot of different ways.

Have fun!

Kristen Dabrowski

ANDREW J. BAKER

Andrew is an upper-class kid at boarding school. His parents are technically together but rarely in the same state at the same time. He has an older sister.

FOUR POINT O

Andrew, semicomic
At school, talking to friends.

OK. One cough means true, two means false. If A is the correct answer, press one finger to your temple like so. *(Demonstrates.)* B is two fingers to your temple and so on. To indicate that we're moving to the next question, stretch like you're yawning. We're always half asleep in Farber's class anyway. And, for God's sake, try to look casual. Like you're thinking. Last time, you couldn't be more obvious, *Ryan.* It's a miracle we weren't caught. We can't take that chance again.

Once again, if I get an A average, in case anyone has forgotten, *I will get a new car of my choice.* That means beer runs, that means girls in the backseat. Get my drift? Do you need me to say it again? Now don't mess this up. I'm counting on you. We have to work together if we're going to pull this off. Let's make this happen, men.

FOR THE RECORD

Andrew, dramatic
At school, talking to a teacher.

Listen, I didn't want to point this out, Mr. Farber, but my parents pay your salary. They make twenty times what you make, I'm sorry to say. I point this out because they are not going to be happy about you reporting this so-called rule breaking. They expect me, fully expect me, to go to Princeton. This little situation could potentially change that. I'm sure the Dean would agree. I'd be happy to mention it to him next time he plays golf with my dad and me.

I'm sorry to be such a—well, you would call me a punk, wouldn't you?—-but these things have to be said. The truth is an ugly thing. You always tell us, correctly, that life is unfair. It is, isn't it, Mr. Farber? This is an ugly and unfair world. But one where my academic record has to remain absolutely clean. Immaculate.

I'm serious, sir. This is no joke. *(Beat.)* You can't do this! You are going to be very, very sorry.

HOT NIGHT

Andrew, comic
At his dorm, talking to his friends.

I am so sick. That was an excellent party, Graves. Seriously excellent. You really came through for us, buddy. Why didn't you tell us that your sister is hot? And her friends . . . You are a lucky man, Graves. I'm not going to be able to walk for a week. I can't even remember getting home! Someone tell me if I had as good a time as I think!

No. Be serious. No, man, be serious! Don't mess with my head. This is not a good day. Tell it like it happened.

I did not spend the night sleeping on the bathroom floor with your dog! No way! I remember a hot chick. A brunette bombshell.

Stop it now. I mean it. No way did it go down like that. I hate you guys. I really do. You're full of it. Don't even talk to me.

PLANS

Andrew, comic
At school, talking to a friend.

Politics. Definitely politics. Can't you just see it? Kissing babies, shaking hands, some society girl who went to Vassar on my arm and a babe waiting at a hotel? That's the life. You just smile and say speeches other people wrote for you. I could really enjoy being a figurehead.

Why do you ask stupid questions, Schwartz? If it was a time of war, I'd bomb the hell out of the troublemakers. You really are naïve.

People would too vote for me! I'm charming, in case you haven't noticed. People love me. Everyone loves me. Name one person who doesn't. *(Beat.)* He's jealous. Name someone else. *(Beat.)* Again, jealous. Name someone else. *(Beat.)* Are you kidding? She *loves* me. Sometimes I don't even know why I talk to you, Schwartz. It's a good thing you're so funny, that's all I can say.

UNSPEAKABLE

Andrew, comic
At school, talking to a girl.

Hi. I couldn't help noticing. You were looking at me, right?
Thought so. Do you want to go somewhere? It's a nice night.
We can get away from the noise. *(Beat.)* Oh. You like this song?
No, really. You *like* it? This is very possibly the worst song ever
written! The lyrics are clichéd and banal; the vocal performance,
pathetic, whiny and synthetic; the tune is—You *really* like this
song? The one playing now? My God. You are cute, but your
taste is awful.

Come on, come on. No offense. Really. Don't walk away. Come
on, you're really cute. You have terrible taste, but you're cute.
Aw, come on. Don't be like that. Can't we all just get along?
Listen, I think we've got the start of something great here, you
and me. I really feel like we've got some chemistry, don't you?

Let's go outside. We can talk better out there. Or suck face.
Whatever.

Come back! We were getting somewhere then!

HOMECOMING DAY

Andrew, dramatic
At school, talking to his mother.

Mom, don't touch me. My hair is fine! Don't . . . pick at me. You're making me look like an idiot in front of my friends. You're making yourself look like an idiot, too. Just contain yourself. You don't mind not talking to me for months at a time, so stop pretending you're so happy to see me! If you missed me so much, you could pick up the phone sometimes.

Do you see what you're doing to me? *I'm* sounding like the mother here. Why am I the parent in this relationship? Just . . . just take a Valium or whatever. Let's not pretend to be what we're not. We are pleasantly civil. Not some loving family. So let's cut the crap.

So where's Dad anyway? What's so important that he couldn't come see me for one day? Another merger? A golf game?

Don't answer that, Mom. I don't want to hear the answer. Fix your makeup and let's get on with this charade.

PULLED OVER

Andrew, dramatic
On the highway, talking to a police officer.

Officer, this car is *new*. Know what I mean? I had no choice.
Just making sure I got my money's worth. You have to test her
out, you know? So, how about you let me go just this one time.
I promise I won't do it again. The car company just kept say-
ing, "Can do zero to sixty in six seconds," so I had to check it
out. Consumer fraud and all that. The car company said,
"Smooth ride even at high speeds and in off-road conditions."
What's a guy to do? They make it so you want to know.

Honestly, I don't have the money to pay for a ticket. I'm a kid.
Can't you just give me a warning this time? My dad will kill
me if I get a ticket; I just *got* the car. I really won't do it again.

Don't pretend like you've never done the same thing! Give me
a break. Don't get so high and mighty on your one ounce of
power. It's pathetic. You're pathetic. Just give me the freakin'
ticket, Officer Major Pig.

You cannot give me another ticket. What the hell! I'll get you
fired, if it's the last thing I do!

THE MOVES

Andrew, comic
At school, talking to a girl.

Hi. Hi, there. I'm Andrew. We met a while back through your brother? Maybe you don't remember. I'm Andrew. Did I already say that? Well . . . yeah. So . . . you're here to see Greg? That's really nice. Will you be staying here for a while? *(Beat.)* The weekend? Great! That's great. For you. And your brother.

Can I show you around or anything? Give you a tour? You're Mary, right? Greg's been hiding you. I bet he didn't show you the new facilities, did he? The theater and the science labs . . . Greg's great, a great, great guy, but he can be forgetful, can't he? Good old Greg. So, are you hungry? Greg shouldn't have left you on your own like this. Not very gentlemanly of him. Can I escort you to the dining hall? *(Beat.)* No, no, of course you can take care of yourself—I didn't mean to say—

Uh, I didn't mean to . . . whatever I did. I just wanted to know if you're hungry. No? OK. Well. OK. So. I'll go now. *(Beat.)* OK. Really . . . nice seeing you. *(Beat.)* Fine, fine! I'll go away now. Jeez, you are cold!

AFTER THE CRASH

Andrew, dramatic
On the side of a deserted road, talking to a friend.

Talk to me, Schwartz! Schwartz, I am talking to you! Jesus! I can't get my phone to work. Where the hell are we? Come on, Schwartz, I can't do this on my own! You're the sensible one! I'm the stupid, careless one!

OK, get your head together, Andrew. What can you do? What can you do. Why won't my phone work? What's the point of these things if they don't work in an emergency! Come on, Schwartz. Just wake up. Wake up! Wake up and tell me you *knew* I was driving too fast in that annoying know-it-all way of yours. You know you want to. Listen, I'll admit it. You were right. I was driving too fast and I'm careless and I'm an idiot. OK? Happy? So wake up already! You have to be OK, Schwartz. Work with me here. We're a team, remember? Come on! Jesus, Schwartz! Why are you always so stubborn? You can't be hurt or dead or anything. Listen to me. Your mom is going to freak and neither of us want to see that, right? You're always complaining how she nags you too much. Just wait 'til she hears about this. Think about it. And I'll fail out of school. You know you get me through my classes. And . . . come on, Schwartz! Jesus!

MISTAKE NO. 386

Andrew, dramatic
At a hospital, talking to his friend's mother.

Mrs. Schwartz, I'm really sorry. Really, really sorry. I know that's not good enough. You should be really mad at me. I'd be mad at me. I *am* mad at me. But Schwartz—Joel—he's gonna be OK, the doctors said. So, I'm just trying to look on the bright side, for Joel's sake. But . . . but I just wanted you to know how sorry I am. I mean, he's great. He's like my best friend. If it weren't for Schwartz, well, I'd be nowhere. He keeps me sane and out of trouble (as much as he can), and I get him out of his shell.

Did you know he's seeing a girl named Mary? Mary Graves. She's really pretty and nice. She wouldn't give me the time of day, of course, but she saw Schwartz's good qualities right away—

No, she's not Jewish. I don't think. But . . . but maybe I'm wrong. I am wrong. I think they're just friends. Yeah. Forget I ever said it. Did I mention that Joel is far and away the best student in our physics class?

He's going to be OK. And . . . I'm just really, really sorry.

RICK VASS

Rick is a know-it-all motormouth. He has an answer for everything and everybody. Rick lives at home with his parents and two younger sisters in the suburbs.

MEATLOAF FRIDAY

Rick, comic
At school, talking to a friend.

My stomach is killing me. What was in that meatloaf? I knew I shouldn't have had it. I knew it, and I ate it anyway. The worst part is, I'm still hungry. I could eat another plate of it. What is wrong with me? I'll eat anything. I mean it. Put me on one of those reality shows. I'd eat the head off a live rat, whatever. God, just thinking about how disgusting I am makes me sick. Not sick enough, but sick.

Oh, man. My guts are eating themselves. I think I might die. I'm sweating, aren't I? What are the symptoms of a heart attack? I feel like I'm having one. Oh, God. I'm dying. Take me, God. Take me now.

Oh! Wait. Something just happened there. A . . . shift. I feel better. I feel much better. I'm going to get more meatloaf. Lend me a dollar.

Don't be a jerk, man! Give me a dollar!

URBAN LEGEND

Rick, comic
In a car, talking to his girlfriend.

You know once I parked in this very same area. And it was very dark outside. There was no one at all around. Just me and some girl I totally don't care about anymore since I met you. And we were, well, let's not talk about that part, but we were in the car. Talking about . . . nature. And then we heard this sound—

No, it was not a man with a hook! Don't interrupt. I'm telling a story here. So, there was this sound. And we stopped . . . talking about nature and she was like, "What was that? Did you hear something?" And I was like, "No, I don't think so. Let's keep talking about nature." And she was like, "No, really. I heard something. Would you check it out?" And I was like, "Hell, no, why would I do that?" But she was going on and on, so I unlocked the door—

No! There was not a man with a hook! Aren't you listening? Fine. I'll just jump to the end. There was a squirrel and it had a necklace in its mouth and *it was my mother's necklace*. Isn't that a weird story?

Fine. Let's shut up and talk about nature.

ENLIGHTENMENT

Rick, comic
At school, talking to his gym teacher.

Mr. Cheng, I'm pretty sure this yoga thing is wrong. The human body is not supposed to do this stuff. I don't actually think I need to explore other consciousnesses, or whatever you said. I mean, if girls want to work themselves into pretzels, that's fine. I'm not here to tell other people what to do. But this isn't . . . manly.

Well, I do think there's a little chance it might make me gay now that you mention it, Mr. Cheng. I'm not saying definitely. But it's possible, isn't it? Straight guys don't care about their bodies. They just know if they've got a beer gut they need to make more money. It's a whole system. But gay guys, well, they need to think about looking hot and being flex—Can we stop this conversation? I'm getting really uncomfortable here. But if it's all the same to you, I'll just do push-ups for the rest of the period.

MISS RIGHT NOW

Rick, comic
At school, talking to his girlfriend.

So, baby, wanna go to my pleasure palace? By pleasure palace, I mean the basement of my house. And by pleasure, I mean doing dirty things. And by dirty things, I mean you doing my laundry. Kidding! Just kidding! So, what do you say? Want to come over to my house tonight? Extreme kickboxing is on.

Yes? You *do* want to watch extreme kickboxing? You know there's blood involved. *(Beat.)* I'm . . . surprised. I think I might be impressed. But then again, usually when I suggest extreme kickboxing, girls would do anything so they don't have to watch it. Well, practically anything. And you . . . huh. You *like* extreme kickboxing. That's . . . cool. But can we at least make out during the commercials?

You are one hell of a girl. I mean that.

PERSPECTIVE

Rick, comic
At home, talking to his mother.

I was thinking. Why do they say "morbidly obese"? It's not that morbid, being fat. Morbid is when you're obsessed with death, right? Being fat is not a death wish. It's a wish for more fried chicken and Cheez Doodles. Sure, you could die, but you're not hoping for it. How come they don't say people who, like, bungee jump are "morbidly adventurous"? Because that makes sense. They are groovin' on the possibility of death. But fat people? No way. They're living in the moment.

How come Americans are so fat, anyhow? That's all anyone talks about. Now people saying we're shallow, I get that. Because who cares if you're fat? Get over it. How can people claim to be tolerant and not dig fat folks? They are just loving life. We should celebrate them.

So when I said that you're "heavy" the other day, Mom, it was actually a compliment, see?

PEDALING BACKWARDS

Rick, dramatic
At home, talking to his sister and his mother.

Isabelle, what the hell's wrong with you? I heard Mom brought you to the doctor because you've been whining so much. Why can't you just suck it up like the rest of us? Being a teenager sucks. Get over it. So stop whining already! And I am not going to go get you a Coke! Do it your damn self!

You're making it up. Lyme disease. You have Lyme disease. Don't trees get that? Give me a break. I'm not stupid, you know.

Stop complaining. "No one believes me! Boo-hoo!" Maybe if you weren't such a whiner we'd listen more.

What do you mean, "Do whatever she wants"? Mom, you can't say that. She's a fourteen-year-old girl. If I give her an inch, she'll take a mile. *(Beat.)* She's not faking? She has some disease?

Well—are you serious? Can I catch it? *(Beat.)* I'm . . . really sorry, Izzy. But don't push it.

THE THIN LETTER

Rick, dramatic
At home, talking to his mother.

I finally got that letter from Notre Dame. Yeah. I didn't get in. No.

It's OK. I mean, it's not OK, not at all. I just don't understand. I have what it takes to go there. And, of course, the letter says all that stuff about "a record number of applications" this year, but they just say that to make you feel like less of a loser, which, of course, it doesn't.

But it shouldn't matter! I get decent grades. I have done all kinds of stupid activities. I just want to get into a decent school and not have to go to a loser one. And I've talked about this for so long with my friends—about how we're all going to go there— that I'm going to look like a complete idiot when I tell them I got *rejected*. I hate that word. I'm a reject.

Do you know how that makes me feel, Mom? I'm a loser. My life is all downhill from here. *(Beat.)* I know Isabelle is sick and there are people worse off in the world. Do you think that makes me feel better? Now I feel like a double loser. Can't I just complain for five minutes ever?

ULTIMATUM

Rick, dramatic
At school, talking to his girlfriend.

Why does everyone pay attention to Max? I'm funnier than he is. I am. Just because he's going to Harvard doesn't make him funnier or smarter than me. Girls even like him now. Like they know that he's going to be making more money than all of us soon. Can't we get in just a few years before the power-money vortex sucks us in? Of course, that's not true. It's sucking us in all the time. Who has the best car? Who has a pool in their backyard? Who comes back from vacation with a tan because they went to Bermuda? It's not fair. I'm never gonna be that person. I'm just a regular guy. You like me more than him, right, Cheryl?

Thanks. *(Beat.)* Yeah, I feel a little better now. Promise me you'll never talk to him. *(Beat.)* Why not? I thought you liked me better. If that's true, then it won't matter. *(Beat.)* You don't *have* to talk to him. So what's it going to be, me or him?

THE BREAKUP

Rick, semicomic
At school, talking to his ex-girlfriend.

Know what? I never liked you. And I kissed Brenda one time when we were going out. So there. *(Beat.)* Yes, I said, "So there." So what? *(Beat.)* I am not immature. I think you're immature because you're going out with my mortal enemy, just to spite me. Now *that's* immature. Just because of where he's going to college. That's shallow. You're a shallow, immature person, Cheryl. I'm sorry to say it. I expected better of you.

Don't tell lies. You were *so* into me the whole time we were going out. Don't even pretend you weren't. I was just going along with the whole relationship thing because that's what I thought you did. Having a girlfriend and all. But now I see that playing the field is the way to go. So you enjoy your pimply-faced, hairy-butt boyfriend. I'm going to be partying and hooking up with every hot girl in college next year. I've never felt freer or more alive in my life.

Hasta la vista, baby.

THE MAKEUP

Rick, semicomic
At school, talking to his ex-girlfriend.

I'm sorry, too. It was a lie. I wasn't happy. *(Beat.)* No, I made that up. I didn't make out with Brenda Cunningham while we were going out. No way. I wouldn't do that to you. I was just mad because you were talking to that jerk Max. *(Beat.)* I guess I was a *little* jealous. But not really. I was more . . . betrayed. You know I hate that guy! I asked you not to talk to him. As a favor to me. And what do you do? You went right up and talked to him. That hurt, Cheryl. I have to tell ya, that was downright bitchy.

I'm not telling you what to do! It was a *favor*, Cheryl. I asked this one thing of you. It's not too much to ask. *(Beat.)* Well, yeah, I still don't want you to talk to him! He's after you and I hate him. Isn't that reason enough? I thought you wanted to get back together. *(Beat.)* Don't be like this. You know I'm better than him or you would never have come back. Come on, Cheryl. You know you like me best. Admit it. You looooove me. You dig me so much you can't even stand it. Admit it! *(Beat.)* Of course, I like you. *(Beat.)* Don't start with the "forever and ever" stuff. We're in high school, for Chrissake.

Fine! We're broken up again! And don't come crawling back!

TYLER KREMBOLD

Tyler is smart. Really smart. He's already in his senior year of college, but is socially immature. Tyler lives with his mother in a large city.

PLANS

Tyler, semicomic
At home, talking to his mother.

Mom, I'm going out. *(Beat.)* Just out! Why do I always have to tell you? I'm in *college*, Mom. I can take care of myself.

I don't exactly know where I'm going. I'm just going. I don't want to be here in this apartment at the moment. I need to clear my head. Be *by myself*. Satisfied? I'll be back in a few hours. I'll bring my cell phone, OK? So if someone tries to murder me or something, I'll give you a call.

You're killing me, Mom. Killing me. Can't you focus on your work or something now?

Fine. I'm going to the park to play chess. OK? And after that I'm going to smoke crack and pick up transvestite hookers.

Jeez—kidding! Get a sense of humor, Mom.

FLYING SOLO

Tyler, semicomic
At school, talking to his professor.

I don't need a mentor, Professor. I'm OK on my own. I like figuring things out for myself. If someone tells you how to do things, then you don't understand why they work how they do. You can't get the logic behind it. If I work slower than other people, that's OK with me. I've had enough of excelling beyond my years.

I know that's a little strange. I appreciate the offer and all. But I'm already a freak. If I get smarter faster, I'll really be in trouble. Everyone's already way older than me in school. The women in bio lab are *old*. Or old*er* I should say. They're *women*. Do you know what I mean? To be honest, it's a little awkward. If I could go backwards, I would. So if it's all the same to you, I'd like to struggle a little bit.

Listen, could you not tell my mom about this? I'd really appreciate it.

CAGED

Tyler, semicomic
In line for the movies, talking to his mother.

Don't. Please. We're in public. And it's disgusting. No, Mom.
Back off. I'm serious. It's not even dermatologically sound. I'll
do it myself later. Do *not* pop my zit.

No, I don't want cover-up to conceal it. I know it's not pretty,
but it's there. So, who cares. Am I that grotesque to you now?
Can't you just ignore it?

When are you going to face up to the fact that I'm an adult? I
can pop my own zits, if I choose to. In fact, let's go to separate
movies. I'm going to go see an action film. We'll get out at about
the same time anyhow.

I don't care if I have to sit by myself. Being by myself doesn't
bother me. In fact, I welcome it. I don't have to think about
making anyone happy. I think it bothers you, being alone. But,
Mom, I *am* going to have to go off on my own someday soon.
Maybe you should be a little less protective and get used to it.

FAKING IT

Tyler, comic
Before class, talking to a girl.

(Lying.) Yeah, I'm in this class. I just never bothered to come. I've been drunk all semester. Partying with my frat brothers. Which frat? Ha, ha. I can't even remember.

This is Life Drawing, right? *(Beat.)* Yeah, I'm into art. Absolutely. I'm a dedicated artist. *(Beat.)* The human form is amazing, isn't it? So . . . who will we be drawing today, Anna? A naked woman, I'm assuming, of course. *(Beat.)* No? A partially clothed woman? Like draped with scarves or something? *(Beat.)* A man. An old man. Are you kidding me? Are you absolutely sure? *(Beat.)* Sure, sure, I'd love to see your drawing of him.

(Forces himself to look.) Oh, God. Man, he's old and wrinkled and so, so naked. That is wrong. *(Beat.)* I mean, I'm sure you really captured his spirit. Your picture is . . . great. You're very talented. Listen, I just remembered, I have somewhere to be. Maybe I can catch up with you later? Maybe we could talk about how great art is some more. I just love art.

Oh, God, he's coming in. I've gotta go. I, uh, need a drink.

SECOND STRING

Tyler, dramatic
At home, talking to his mother.

Mom, any chance Dad will come visit on my birthday? It's OK if he doesn't. I know he has his new family to deal with. But we haven't seen him in a while. Could I give him a call?

Why not? You're always trying to keep me from talking to Dad. Are you jealous or something? *(Beat.)* No, not of his new family. Jealous because we get along so well. We're so alike, Dad and me. *(Beat.)* Mom, of course I see Dad less so he gets on my nerves less. I know that. But we still . . . He's still my dad. And I want to see him this year.

He *will* come. He owes me at this point. He knows that. *(Beat.)* Don't be so scared all the time. You're too overprotective. And you're too ready to think negative things about Dad. Just because we don't live with him anymore and he has his other family and sometimes he forgets things, doesn't mean we're not his family still. I'm calling him now.

'NOID NERD

Tyler, semicomic
In the lab, talking to himself.

Is someone there? *(Laughs.)* I'm losing it. It's just so creepy being in the lab after everyone's gone. Isn't it? *(Beat.)* Hello?

What's wrong with me? No one's here. Who would want to be here? No one! To nearly everyone on earth, this is the most boring place imaginable. Why am I talking to myself? I don't know. OK; I'm going to stop now.

However, it is possible that I've somehow unearthed some kind of medical secret. Who would want it? The FBI? They would probably just ask. Maybe someone just hates me. Maybe it's some serial killer that only attacks guys who go to college early. He's madly jealous because he never got in at all. Why am I still talking to myself?

(Long beat.)

Who are you? Show yourself! I happen to be holding a highly combustible liquid at the moment. I won't hesitate to use it as a biological weapon! Hello?

LIKE IT IS

Tyler, comic
At home, talking to his mother.

Can't you support me in this? This is an anthropological study, Mom! And, do you know what? I don't gave a—damn!—-what you think about it! So there!

You didn't like that word? Well, just you wait. In fact, not only am I going to use curse words now, I'm going—gonna—use bad grammar and ghetto slang, bitch.

No, Mom, I meant it in slang terms, not literal terms. It's different. It means just "woman." I just want you to understand, yo. I don't fit in with other people my age, you dig? And a huge part of that is how formally I speak. Whenever I try to use more casual language—that other people use every day—I sound *wrong*. That's merely from lack of familiarity and use, I believe. See? I should never have said "I believe." It sounds absurd. I should have said "straight up" or something.

This isn't bullcrap, Mom. This is important. I'm way behind the times. It's not rad. I'll never be wicked cool, but I have to try.

IGNORANCE

Tyler, comic
At school, talking to a female classmate.

Sharks aren't actually scary. No, they're not. They serve a necessary biological function. They keep fish populations in check. And they only bite people when they swim in murky water or when they're in a school of fish. Sharks don't *want* to eat people. People are ignorant. If you put yourself in a shark's natural habitat you have to expect that something might happen. Sharks don't just attack people. They take a little test nip to see what's dangling in the water. They can't help it if they have genetically super-sharp teeth and happen to rip your legs off. Nearly always, after they've realized they've chomped on the wrong thing, they just go away.

Now, don't you feel silly? *(Beat.)* Well, I just mean because you thought sharks were scary. Now that you've learned more about them, they seem quite safe, don't they? *(Beat.)* No? Why not? I don't get it. It makes perfect sense to me.

Girls don't make any sense. You're just not logical.

YOU DA MAN

Tyler, comic
At school, talking to a female classmate.

Remember when I said I didn't like you like that? I think . . .
I think I didn't mean it. I think I do like you. Like that.

Why did I say that? Because . . . I don't know. I just didn't know
you like I know you now. *(Beat.)* I know it was only a week
ago. I guess I've just been thinking about it. And . . . between
the two of us . . . I was sort of freaked out by your . . . for-
wardness. I guess I'm not used to it. You're so . . . direct. It's
refreshing, though. I'm not too good at reading signals. It's a
guy thing. So, you kind of caught me off guard. But what do
you say we . . . I don't know . . . maybe we could . . .

Sure. Friday at six. Dinner and a movie. Sure. That works fine.
But listen, do you think maybe . . . sometimes—

Of course I can complete a sentence. It's just that . . . maybe . . .
could I sometimes make some of the decisions? I mean, not
today or tomorrow or Friday or anything, but someday.

DRAFTED

Tyler, dramatic
At home, talking to his mother.

Is this allowed? Do they know about me? I'm not a fighter. I'm a brain. I couldn't possibly! I don't even know if I believe in this cause. Or even in war in general! Is this for real?

And I have no choice? That doesn't seem right. How can I have no choice? I thought this was a free country. That's what everyone says. It's all a lie. Look, I don't want to do this. I'm serious. I'm scared. I'm sure this is not what I was supposed to do in my life. And if I die? If I get killed? I haven't lived at all. Not even for a kid my age. I haven't done anything.

Can I . . . I'm going to go abroad. Run. I have to. I don't care if you don't approve. I can't do this.

THEO MARTINEZ

Theo is a musician. He's not very good in school and struggles to keep up. Theo lives with his mother, father, and three sisters in a large city.

THE BIG CHECK

Theo, comic
At school, talking to a friend.

I was just thinking about this stuff like the lottery and things where people get those big checks. You know? Where a bunch of guys show up with this check that's, like, bigger than a person, for a million dollars or whatever. Wouldn't it be funny to steal that check? I mean, it's so big. You just see those lottery guys walking down the street and—*zoink!*—just pull it out from under their arm. Then it would be like, "Hey, look at me! I'm a millionaire!" Is there a bank that takes those checks? Or what would one of those check-cashing places do with it? I bet they'd take it. It's kind of hard to be sneaky if the police are hunting for a criminal with a big check, though.

Didn't some celebrity's mom win the lottery? That's so wrong. Like she needs it. She should leave the lottery to poor people. Rich people are so greedy. I bet all their checks are big billboard-size checks. Pigs. But now I think I know what I want to do for a living. I'll be a modern-day Robin Hood. Stealing big checks from the rich and keeping them for myself. It's a greedy world, man.

MORNING BLUSH

Theo, comic
At home, talking to his mother.

Oh, Mom, you didn't! Why? Why? Why couldn't you just leave it alone? Why didn't you use *your* room? Now I have to suffer! *(Beat.)* You're joking, right? You think this is a *success*? No way, Mom. Seriously. This is no good. I don't know what the hell show you've been watching, but this is *not* a good design for a guy's room. Flowers, Mom? Flowers? *(Beat.)* You are banned from watching the TV. You do whatever they say. They do flower arranging, and you do it. They cover pillows with— what *is* this anyway? And I don't want to see you rummaging in other people's trash again. *(Beat.)* I don't care if that's what they did on TV! Aren't you listening? It's embarrassing. You're not allowed to watch anymore, Mom. Real people don't do this stuff. And they certainly don't do it to their son's room. This is a crime. Seriously. I'd be within my rights to arrest you. A crime against humanity.

You'd better pick up another gallon of paint because I'm not spending a single day in a pink room, Mom. *(Beat.)* It is not Morning Blush, Mom. It's pink. Now get to work. No excuses! You brought this on yourself.

IN CHARGE

Theo, comic
At home, talking to his sister.

Luce, I am sure you are not allowed to go out now. Come on.
Who do you think you're kidding? Mom and Dad did not say
you could go out to see your friends at ten o'clock at night. They
didn't. I'm not stupid. *(Beat.)* Don't say I'm stupid, Lucy. Mom
and Dad aren't here, and that means I'm in charge. And me
being in charge means you do what I want. And you doing what
I want means you do your homework your damn self. And
doing your homework your damn self means you don't go to
your friend's house. Get it?

I am not mean. I am being protective of your stupid ass. Do
you think I enjoy having to tell you what to do? *(Beat.)* Well,
I *don't.* I have better things to do than babysit. Maybe that didn't
occur to you. Now shut up and do your homework.

I don't know what. Just things. I have *things* to do, OK? Now
can you shut your bratty mouth for once?

Oh, come on. You're not allowed to cry. *(Beat.)* It is too a rule.
A new rule. No crying. Aw, jeez. I wouldn't yell at you if you'd
just do your homework. *(Beat.)* Fine, fine. Call Jocelyn and
complain about what a monster I am. But while you're on the
phone, get her to help you with your homework!

THE REFUSAL

Theo, dramatic
At school, talking to a teacher.

No way. No. Way. She cannot—No, I'm sorry. I can't do this.
Isn't there any other way? It's just that . . . this is going to be
so embarrassing. Lauren Mandelbaum has been an annoying
know-it-all (I'm sorry to say it, but it's true) since the day she
was born, Mrs. McKinny. She's been making fun of me since
first grade. If you make her my tutor . . . I just can't do it. Don't
you get it? It's like saying she's right. She's been right all these
years. I would rather die than do that.

It isn't exaggerating. I don't normally come out and say things
like this, at least not to teachers, but I hate that girl. I really
do. She hasn't changed since first grade. I mean, first grade, for
crying out loud! I've always dreamed of being *her* tutor, actually. Is there any way you can make that happen? Even just for
laughs?

I didn't think so. But I'd rather be stupid than humiliated. I
would. So if there's some B or C student who could help me,
that would be fine for me. I mean, anything would help, right?

REGRESSION

Theo, dramatic
At school, talking to a classmate.

That makes no sense. It doesn't. You're a lousy teacher. Just because you're smart doesn't mean you can teach, and boy, oh boy, you cannot teach, sister.

I am not dumb. You're too smart. You're a freak, Lauren. You're going to be like the female Bill Gates or who's that scientist guy in the wheelchair? Stephen Hawking. Right. Him. But without the wheelchair. But plenty weird.

Listen, just do me a favor and shut up? I've had it with you. Believe it or not, I don't get any better at math with you bringing me down. Believe it or not, I'm already pretty hard on myself. Do you think I want to be dumb? Especially in math which guys are supposed to be decent at? So stop being a little bitch, OK?

Jesus, don't cry. It's just like old times, Lauren. Just like first grade. You say something cruel, I say something back, you cry, and I get in trouble. It's been, like, ten years of this stuff, and it is getting boring already! So just quit it.

DISBELIEF

Theo, semicomic
At school, talking to a friend.

No way. She doesn't. That's sick. Lauren Mandelbaum doesn't like me. We've been mortal enemies forever. That's chemically impossible, not to mention stupid. And she's the smartest girl in school, so again, there's no way.

She did not tell Danielle that. Does she even talk to Danielle? I think this is a setup. Someone is trying to play a joke on me. But this one is completely unbelievable, so the joke's on them.

Shhh! She's coming over here, so shut up. It's probably just to talk about my stupid math tutoring. Shhh!

Hi. Yeah. Later. Like usual. I know. You don't have to remind me. I'm not stupid. *(Beat.)* Joe's Pizza? Why would we work there? We always just work in the classroom. *(Beat.)* I *know* I always complain I'm hungry, but that's to make the tutoring end sooner. *(Beat.)* Fine; whatever.

See, she doesn't like me. I hate her and she hates me. End of story.

GENTLEMAN, SCHMENTLEMAN

Theo, comic
Outside school, talking to a classmate.

I am not carrying your pink umbrella for you. I'm not some knight in shining armor. I'm a *guy*. In the twenty-first century. And *guys* don't carry pink things. Unless those *Queer Eye* guys come to my house, it's not gonna happen.

Lauren, you need to stop being bossy. I can't take it. I'm not your boyfriend or anything. I don't care if I'm not a gentleman. I don't like you. I didn't want to come out and say it, especially since you might cry *again*, but there it is. I don't like you.

You don't like me either? Don't lie. People told me you like me. I know you like me or else you wouldn't be so into tutoring me. *(Beat.)* Quit it! You do not "want to help me." That's a load of crap. You are *so* into me.

You are, too! I am *not* getting upset! I just think you should face the truth!

DISCIPLINE

Theo, comic
At home, talking to his sister.

I think the people upstairs are doing voodoo. I peeked into their apartment just now, and the whole place has loads of red candles burning. That lady who lives there kills live chickens. Plus, remember when the ceiling leaked in here because the pipes were overloaded? The water was this brown nasty color. That was blood, Cissy. Blood.

I *am* serious. Mom and Dad don't know it because they don't know about voodoo. I do. I watched a show on TV. Now you had better behave yourself and stop being a brat because those people could take you and sacrifice you. I mean it. *(Beat.)* If you leave the apartment when you're not supposed to, they could get you. Or if you're really bad, I'll give you to the voodoo people. I don't want to, but if you're bad, I won't have a choice. *(Beat.)* Mom and Dad would be mad, but they have me and the other girls, so they'd be OK after a day or two.

Are you going to do your homework now? Shhh! What's that I hear? Doesn't it sound like a chicken is crying upstairs?

PARENTING 101

Theo, comic
At home, talking to his parents.

I did not tell Cissy that gypsies would eat her. *(Beat.)* No, I didn't. Not even close. That kid is cracking up. She never listens. It's hard to watch her after school. She's a little brat. And she's got it all wrong.

They weren't *gypsies*. They were *voodoo* people. I was going to give her to the voodoo people upstairs. *(Beat.)* Why is that bad? I wouldn't do it, and it made her be quiet for the rest of the afternoon. I thought it was pretty effective myself. It was a good idea. You should be proud of me.

What did I do that was bad? She wanted to leave the house. She's not supposed to. So I made sure she didn't. I could just let her do whatever she wants. But I don't. I watch her like I'm supposed to. I'm not even getting paid for this stuff. In fact, I'd suggest you use the voodoo thing yourself sometimes. This is good stuff and I'm giving it to you for free. You should thank me. Or pay me! That would be even better.

SHE'S ALL MIME

Theo, comic
At school, talking to a friend.

I thought girls liked musicians. No girls are into me. At least not the ones I want to be into me. And the ones that are into me—well, let's just say I'm not into them. Girls can be so clingy. You talk to them and they think you're going to marry them or something. And all you hear is, "When am I going to see you next?" "Are you coming to watch me do my homework?" "Will you call me five seconds after school?" Give me a break. It gets to the point where you have nothing to say. There's so much talking required.

I don't have anything to say ever. I don't! It's so much pressure and so boring. They don't realize, it just makes you want to get away from them as soon as possible. Even the possibility of some action doesn't make it worth it. Then you have to do all this explaining. "Why don't you talk to me anymore?" "Don't you like me?" And all you want to do is scream, "Yes! I don't like you! In fact, I hate you!" But you can't because then they'd start crying, and then there would be more talking.

Know what I'd like? A really sexy, mute girlfriend.

MICK MACMILLAN

Mick fights with everyone and enjoys it. Clever but aimless and immature, Mick makes and loses friends quickly. He lives with his parents in a rural area.

SOMETHING TO DO

Mick, comic
At home, talking to a friend.

We need to come up with something new to do. I'm sick of driving in circles. Cruising the neighborhood has lost its appeal. We've knocked down everybody's mailbox and tipped every cow in town. Now what? I am seriously bored.

Wanna dig a hole? I have some shovels out back. *(Beat.)* I don't know why. For something to do. I know! We could dig out a six-foot hole, like a grave, behind someone's house and make a grave stone–type thing with their name on it to freak them out. Or, we could dig out someone's front lawn so when they leave the house in the morning, they'll fall in the hole. Or drive someone's tractor into a ditch we dug.

I just thought it would be a good idea, for a change. If you don't like it, *you* come up with something. *(Beat.)* You can't tip over a horse so shut up now. It will kick you in the head, you idiot.

That's it. I've had it with you. Get over here, so I can kick your ass.

LIKE A HOLE IN THE HEAD

Mick, comic
At home, talking to a friend.

(Holding his hand to the back of his head.) No, I'm OK. Don't get my mom. She'll overreact. It'll stop bleeding soon. She's always going on and on about how we shouldn't wrestle. This will give her an excuse to act like a chicken with its head cut off.

This feels weird. I'm light-headed. It's kind of . . . cool. I feel light as air. So, how does it look? *(Takes his hand away from his head.)* Do I have a big hole in my head or is it OK?

Oh, well. I'll just wear a ball cap to cover it up. Let's go again. I'll bet you I can push you onto the porch in ten seconds.

What, are you scared? *(Beat.)* Then let's go, mama's boy. I'm gonna—

(Faints.)

GUY TALK

Mick, comic
At the hospital, talking to his mother.

I look like I'm sixty. I look like one of those old monks with the weird bald spots. Did they have to shave my head to give me stitches? Or is it just a joke doctors play? It must be excellent to be a doctor. Not the going-to-school-for-years part, but the operating-on-people part. You have total control over them. Plus, it's gross. You get to pull people apart—the skin, the muscles, sawing through bones . . .

You never let me say or do anything, Mom. I don't get it. We're not eating, so why can't I talk about people's guts? If you don't like it, maybe you just shouldn't listen. If I only said things you approved of, I'd talk about flowers and celebrities and wallpaper and stuff. *(Beat.)* Yeah, I bet you would like that, but it's not going to happen. You're probably the only mother on earth who wishes she had a gay son. So sorry to disappoint you, Mom.

Well, there's no chance you'll get a daughter; you're too old to have more kids now. So you have to make do with me and I'm a *guy*. And I happen to be interested in what it's like to cut into people. So go to your happy place and think about flowers, Mom, because I'm wanting to talk about gore.

RED, WHITE, AND PINK

Mick, semicomic
At home, talking to his mother.

Uh, Mom, we have a little problem. You're not gonna like it. I want you to promise you won't get mad. I was trying to help. And I was doing what you told me to do. *(Beat.)* You can't get mad yet. You don't even know what happened. It was just a tiny . . . oversight.

I was washing some clothes. Some light-colored clothes. And, see, there was a red sock. I didn't know. And I told you I'm no good at laundry. It's like my teachers say, I don't pay attention to details. So, you know the rest. You have to go buy me new clothes now. I'm going to need underwear and T-shirts.

Don't even joke about that. You're not funny. I'm not wearing pink underwear. I'll steal money from your wallet and buy new stuff myself. I'm not kidding. Don't be cruel, Mom. If you don't want this kind of thing to happen again, you can just do the laundry yourself. You're good at it, and it's your job anyway.

BANG, BANG

Mick, semicomic
Outside, talking to his best friend.

Do you think you could kill someone? I mean, really kill them? Like, how about a stranger? Someone you don't even know or hate. Do you think you could do that? Would it be easier or harder? And if you die, would you go to heaven or hell? Is hell really that bad? Do you get to do all bad things? In that case, it might be a good time. And if you killed someone, how would you do it? I think I'd shoot someone. Imagine what it's like having a bullet rip through your organs. Bleeding to death.

Go stand over there. Hold one of those cans out in front of you. I'm gonna shoot it out of your hand. I've been practicing. I can do it. Don't be a chicken!

OK! Stand very still! Don't shake! Stand still! OK—here we go! One, two, three—

(Laughs.) That was so funny. You looked so scared! Do you really think I'd do that? Man, are you stupid. You almost deserve to be shot.

ART

Mick, comic
At school, talking to a teacher and his best friend.

(Speaking to his class.) This is called, uh, "Wasteland." It's a glimpse at the future where people will be building stuff out of what we now consider junk like Coke cans, Mountain Dew bottles, and old cell phones. It's also a commentary on our materialistic society. People in the future will say, "They used to just throw this stuff away! If they saved more stuff, we could have a mansion made of old bottles instead of a trailer made of old toilet paper!" And how come there aren't any no-name brands here? There's all Coke and Pepsi-type stuff. It's because we are a messed-up society. And . . . and . . . that's it, Mrs. Maitland.

(Speaking to his friend.) I can't believe I had to dig through the garbage at lunch for *art class*. That was nasty. Do you think Mrs. Maitland bought all that crap? Do you think these other kids actually think the crap they brought in actually means something? You gotta wonder, Ken.

Hey, wait! Could I take this stuff to some fancy gallery and actually sell it? I bet I could. Man, people are suckers.

KEEP AWAY

Mick, comic
At school, talking to his friends.

Give it back to me. Now. I'm serious. This is getting really stupid. Give me back my hat already, guys!

You know I don't like to be without it. Listen, I know where you all live. I'm serious. I'll mess up your stuff. I know exactly what's important to you and where you keep it.

I don't need that hat anyway. I want it, on principle, but I don't *need* it. So keep it, losers.

Seriously, give it back to me now before I pound your skulls in. When you least expect it, I'll pants you in front of the whole school. GIVE IT TO ME!

It makes me feel naked, OK? It's, like, my trademark and I don't want to be without it. You know, you're not funny. Listen, I'm going to nail your moms if you don't stop.

Jesus, I hate you guys!

NEWS TO ME

Mick, dramatic
At home, talking to his parents.

I'm *what*? Is this some kind of joke? You're acting weird.

Good one, Mom and Dad. You had me for a minute there. Give me a break, though. We all have the same color eyes and hair. We look alike. So it was a lame joke when you think about it.

Seriously, are you trying to be funny? Because you get on me for pulling dumb pranks, and this is about the dumbest I've ever heard. I mean, why would you wait until now to tell me? I'm old. This is the kind of thing you tell someone when they're little. And, I would have figured it out by now if it was true.

Stop. You're really starting to make me mad. I don't get this. Is it really true? Be honest this time.

I'm adopted. No kidding. I'm adopted. And you're telling me now? Today? *(Laughs.)* This is a joke, right? You really got me this time. *(Gets serious again.)* I can't believe you guys.

RETRIBUTION

Mick, semicomic
At school, talking to his friends.

Know what I wrote my college essay about? Jeremy's big, fat nipples. "Pink like a mouse's eyes," I wrote, "and big as flying saucers." Then I went into a story about how the Pig Lady in the lunch room lusts after him—

Ow! You punched me! What did you do that for? I was *joking*. Learn to take a joke, man. Damn, that *hurt*, pig boy. What do you think you're doing? You are so dead. If you broke it, you are gonna pay.

You're lucky. I'm not bleeding. You're a complete weenie, Jeremy. You have no sense of humor. *(Beat.)* Don't you get mad at me. If anyone should be mad here, it's me. Cool it! Jeez, did I hurt your feelings, dweeb? Get over it.

Ow! You punched me again! What is wrong with you? Do you feel better now? Are you done? Great. So, are we going to play baseball already or just sit here?

THE PLAN

Mick, comic
At home, talking to his best friend.

Ken, have you actually ever seen anyone get sliced up by a
swather? I just wonder what happens to your bones. Can they
slice your bones, too? I guess it can chop little bones, like fingers, since it can cut through loads of crops. But, like, a leg?
Could it do that?

I'm not planning on finding out. Not firsthand, anyway. I was
just wondering. I'm curious.

How come girls say they hate to be scared, but they secretly
like it? How come they lie about it? And why do we like to be
scared anyhow? Isn't that stupid when you think about it?

What's the scariest movie you know, Ken? I was just thinking
maybe we should have girls over to watch a movie. Lately, I
noticed that every time I say something graphic, let's say, like
the tractor thing, Jenn Watkins grabs onto my arm and begs
me to stop. What do you think she'd grab if we watched a really freaky movie? I'm just thinking I'd like to find out. What
do you think?

JASON SPRATCHER

Jason spends a lot of time trying to work out his image and place in the world. He is a bit of a follower and likes to please people. Jason lives with his mother, his aunt, and his baby cousin in a city.

BAD BOYS

Jason, semicomic
At a diner, talking to a girl.

I didn't say anything. I wasn't talking to you. I wasn't talking at all.

But . . . but since we're talking *now*, can you explain to me why girls like guys who treat them bad? I . . . I just don't get it.

That guy is being a total jerk to you. And you let him. I'm not judging, I'm just saying . . . You know. It's not quite right. I'm sure he's sometimes OK. He must have some good points, right? He's . . . large and his face is . . . large . . . and he speaks the same language as you, which always helps . . .

Anyway, I was just wondering. If you don't mind. I'm just curious.

No, I wasn't talking to your girlfriend! I was just . . . sitting. I'm not . . . I wouldn't . . . I was just . . . How about I just go away now. Please?

POINTLESS

Jason, semicomic
Outside, talking to his aunt.

Do I really have to wear this? I really don't think people are so hot to pick my pocket. I'm a kid. Everyone knows I have no money. And if they did try to steal my money, well, you only gave me five dollars. Is it really that important?

It's just that . . . this looks like I'm wearing my bladder on the outside. And it's what old men wear. It's . . . not what young people do. It's not . . . cool. If that makes any sense. It's just kind of humiliating. I mean, it's called a fanny pack. Even the name is embarrassing.

This vacation sucks. I mean it. I'm sorry if I'm not being nice, but it's a stone-cold fact. We're visiting colleges *you* want me to go to. Not ones that interest me. Then I have to wear stupid clothes to "make a good impression." As if I care about my impression. If they don't like me for me, I don't want to be here.

Everyone's staring at me with this pig's bladder around my waist! Let's go home already!

SIDE EFFECTS

Jason, dramatic
At home, talking to his mother.

This new medicine makes me feel really weird. It's like the world is too . . . moving too fast or something. My heart is, like, racing. I'm not sure this is right, Mom. I'm just feeling a little nuts.

I know it's going to feel different than before, but . . . my mouth is so dry. It's just . . . I wouldn't say anything if I didn't feel really . . .

No, no. I don't need to go to the hospital. I'm fine. I don't know. Maybe I'm supposed to feel this way. But . . . do *you* feel like this? I think I liked it better when I was depressed. Look at me; I'm sweating! And I'm just standing still! Is this what the rest of my life will be like? I'll be one of those crazy, butt-scratching, sweating guys who yells at people all the time!

I'm gonna puke. Mom, this is *wrong*.

PROBLEMS

Jason, dramatic
Outside, talking to his father.

Dad, your answer to everything is yelling. I mean, you don't scare me, I know you don't mean anything by it, but . . . you make me feel like everything's my fault.

See? Like now. I'm just trying to express myself, calmly, and you start yelling. The whole neighborhood can hear you, you know. Do you want to terrorize them, too?

OK, I take back the word "terrorize." But you know what I mean. Can't you—

Where are you going? What do you mean, you're "walking it off"? We were having a conversation! Fine. Just go. Whatever. Why do you have to be like this? I'm glad you don't live with us anymore! You're a lousy dad!

SKIN DEEP

Jason, dramatic
At school, talking to a friend.

Are you serious? She's cool. And sexy. It doesn't matter what she looks like. *(Beat.)* You know what I mean. It doesn't matter what color her skin is.

I didn't think anybody thought like that anymore. Are you serious? *(Beat.)* I do not have a responsibility to my race. I don't even know what that means. It doesn't make sense. People are people. If you like them, it doesn't matter what they look like.

You think *I'm* racist? Why? *(Beat.)* I'm not ashamed or trying to be what I'm not. That doesn't make sense. I *do* like people of my race. I'm talking to you, aren't I? It's just that I don't *only* like people of my race. And this girl . . .

I didn't know you were like this, man. Listen, I like her and I'm going to ask her to the prom no matter what. So just stay out of my face.

PROVERBIAL SLAP IN THE FACE

Jason, semicomic
At school, talking to a friend.

I have a really good time with you. It's nice to have a friend who's a girl, Kat. But . . . I also like you. You know, *like you* like you. What do you think about that? I mean, I know I'm not the most popular guy or the toughest or the smartest or the most athletic or anything, but we're friends, right? You like me, right? So it makes sense that maybe—

What? No, really. Hold on. Did you just say what I think you said? *(Beat.)* A lesbian. *(Beat.)* Are you just saying that because you don't want to go out with me? Because that is low. You could just say you're not interested. I thought we were friends—

No way! Are you joking then? This is . . . But . . . I thought . . . You're serious. And you've never . . . You're not at all . . . to me? Are you sure?

Of course, we're still friends. I just . . . Do you think maybe you could tell me who else is gay so I don't make this mistake twice? I don't think I could take the humiliation.

REFLECTIONS OF YOU

Jason, comic
In a store, talking to a friend.

I *knew* you were there. Behind the window. I did too know!
That's why I did it—to give you a laugh. I would never check
myself out and pick stuff out of my teeth in front of a window.
I know better than that. Listen, you told me to meet you here,
right? So . . .

No, I didn't know you'd be sitting *right* there. I just figured . . .
Let's stop talking about this. This is stupid. Look, I care about
my appearance, OK? I was just making sure . . . I had an everything bagel. I was checking for seeds, OK? Is that so wrong?
Wouldn't it be worse to be walking around with black things
in my teeth?

No, I'm not falling for that. There is not a poppy seed in my
teeth. You're full of it. I won't look. No. No. You're lying.
(Beat.) OK, fine, you win! Where's a mirror? Come on, someone might see me like this!

THE ITCHY AND SCRATCHY SHOW

Jason, comic
At home, talking to his mother.

(Trying not to scratch.) Mom, can I talk to you? Well, it's just that . . . I've got this thing on my skin and it itches. No, I'd rather not show you. It's not . . . bad . . . it just itches. It's red. I dunno, it could be a bug bite, I guess. Except . . . it's kind of all over.

No, I don't want to show you! I'm not a baby. I just want to go buy something for it. So I want to know what it is and what I should buy.

Don't do this to me, Mom. I'm not two years old. I am not going to pull off my pants to show you my rash thing. It seems like a poison ivy–type thing, but when have I been in poison ivy? Not since I was about ten. So it can't be that. It's kind of driving me crazy, so if you have any ideas . . . Please, Mom. Tell me now.

No! No. I won't. I don't see why it's necessary. Please, Mom. *(Beat.)* OK, fine! *(Starts to unzip his pants.)* I hope you're happy!

CLUB ZERO

Jason, comic
Outside, talking to a friend.

Listen, man, I've done everything you've asked me: get a girl's underwear, take a piece of fruit from the fruit stand, pants a nerd . . . Can't we be done with this already? I'm not even sure I care about any of this anymore. I mean, what does this so-called secret society do anyway? What do you have to offer me?

OK, fine, it wouldn't be a secret then. Come on. When are you going to let me in the group?

I'm in? Seriously? Excellent! So, what do we do now? *(Beat.)* Hang? That's it? *(Beat.)* Well, sure I can look cool. Don't I always? *(Beat.)* We did this before I went through all that initiation stuff. Is this it? I kissed an old lady on the lips for this? Man, you suck. Seriously.

Come on. Let's find a new pledge to haze. I've got to make this worth it somehow.

GRADUATION PARTY

Jason, semicomic
At a friend's house, talking to a friend.

I feel fine. Stop being such a girl about this. Give me another already. I know when I've had enough and I have *not* had enough.

When I get to college, man, I am gonna party. I am *so* gonna party. Just get me some girls and a beer and I'm happy.

My parents . . . Know what? I don't care what my parents think when I get home. Maybe I won't even go home. They treat me like a *kid*. And I am not a kid. Look at me! I am a *man*.

Have I told you I love beer? I love beer. And I love you guys. You're cool. My friends are cool. You're the greatest friends a guy could have. We're still gonna be friends, right? Dudes, we just graduated. Can you believe it? *We just graduated!* This is the best night of my life.

Hold on. Get outta my way; I'm gonna puke.

THE AUTHOR

Kristen Dabrowski is an actress, writer, acting teacher, and director. She received her MFA from The Oxford School of Drama in Oxford, England. The actor's life has taken her all over the United States and England. Her other books, published by Smith and Kraus, include *111 Monologues for Middle School Actors Volume 1*, *The Ultimate Audition Book for Teens 3*, and *20 Ten-Minute Plays for Teens Volume 1*. Currently, she lives in the world's smallest apartment in New York City. You can contact the author at monologuemadness@yahoo.com.